Easy Weekend Crochet

Volume 1

Slipper Boots

Vicki Becker

Copyright © 2016 Vicki Becker. All rights reserved worldwide.

Copyright © 2016 Vicki Becker. All rights reserved worldwide.

No part of this publication may be replicated, redistributed, or given away in any form or by any means, including scanning, photocopying, or otherwise without the prior written consent of the copyright holder.

You have permission to sell items you personally make from the patterns but not for commercial or mass production purposes. You do not, however, have permission to use my photographs to sell your items.

All patterns are sold in good faith. Every effort has been made to ensure that all instructions are accurate and complete.

http://easyweekendcrochet.com

First Printing, 2016
ISBN-13: 978-1507882320
ISBN-10: 1507882327

Printed in the United States of America

Contents

Contents 3
Introduction 4
General Instructions 5
    Gauge 5
    Understanding Symbols 5
    How to read patterns with multiple sizes 5
    Motif Centers 5
    Using stitch or place markers 5
    Standard Yarn Weight System 5
Helpful Hints 6
    Changing colors 6
    Using more than one color 6
    Make your slippers non-slip! 6
Abbreviations 7
Crochet Terms 8
Skill Level Definitions 9
Special Stitches 11
Pretty in Pink 15
Boots With The Fur 19
Ribbed Lounging Boots 25
Cozy Bobble Boots 31
Houndtooth Check Boots 37
Simply Striped Boots 43
More Needlework Books by Vicki Becker 49
Conclusion 58

Introduction

Slipper Boots is the first book in the Easy Weekend Crochet series. These crocheted slippers are quick and easy projects that you can complete in a weekend or less. Slipper boots keep your feet warm and toasty and are perfect for lounging and snuggling. Crochet these comfy cozy boots for yourself or as a gift for someone special.

The slipper boots are crocheted from the top down using basic crochet stitches. Separate instructions are given for the cuffs so you can easily make them shorter or taller and customize the color. Bulky yarns and large hooks are used which makes the slippers quick to make. You should already know basic crochet stitches, how to read patterns, and whip stitch crochet together. I have included instructions for stitches you may not be familiar with and explain how to place markers. The patterns include six different styles of slipper boots for children and adults in eight sizes.

Vicki

General Instructions

Gauge

Gauge is determined by the tightness or looseness of your work and will affect the finished size of your project. Make a small section of the pattern before starting your project to check the gauge.

Understanding Symbols

As asterisk (*) indicates that the directions immediately following are to be repeated the given number of times in addition to the original.

Parenthesis is used to set off a group of instructions worked a number of times or in a particular stitch. For example, "(3 dc, ch 1, 3 dc) in each corner" or "(3 dc, ch 3) 3 times".

How to read patterns with multiple sizes

When crocheting or knitting a pattern with multiple sizes parentheses are often used to include additional information for other sizes. For example, if the instructions read chain 12 (14, 16), you would chain 12 for size small, 14 for medium, and 16 for large.

Motif Centers

After making a center ring I always crochet over the tail end of the yarn. I can then pull the end of the yarn to make a nice tight center.

Using stitch or place markers

For crochet you need either an open stitch marker or one that opens and closes. Because they can be removed at any time, open stitch markers are perfect for attaching to crochet stitches. Closed stitch markers are used for knitting and don't work for crochet. You can purchase stitch markers or you can use a safety pin or paper clip. Crochet patterns direct you where to place a marker and can use the abbreviation PM or place marker.

Standard Yarn Weight System

Most yarn and thread now come with a weight number on the wrapper. I provide the weight number of the yarn or thread I used to design each pattern. This makes it much easier to make substitutions.

Helpful Hints

Changing colors

To change color in single or double crochet you always work the last two loops on the hook off with the new color.

For single crochet, pull up a loop in the current color you are using, draw the new color through the last two loops on the hook to complete the single crochet stitch.

For double crochet, yarn over, pull up a loop in the current color you are using, draw through two loops, draw the new color through the last two loops on the hook to complete the double crochet stitch.

Using more than one color

Capital letters A, B, C, D, etc, are used to indicate different yarn colors that are to be used. When only two colors are used and one of them is intended to be used as the main or dominant color the terms Main Color (MC) and Contrasting Color (CC) are used.

Make your slippers non-slip!

I used white so you can see what the puffy paint looks like!

Knitted or crocheted slippers are very slippery on laminate, hard wood, or tile floors. There are several methods to make them non-slip.

I use Puffy Paint. You can find puffy paint just about anywhere that sells craft supplies. Just dot some on the slipper bottom or make some squiggly lines or swirls.

Available on-line is Regia ABS Latex or Efco Sock Stop.

Abbreviations

Crochet Abbreviations			
beg	begin, beginning	MC	main color
bet	between	mm	millimeter(s)
BL	back loop(s)	oz	ounce
Bpdc	back post double crochet	p	picot
CA	color A	PM	place marker
CB	color B	pat(s) or patt	pattern(s)
CC	contrasting color	rem	remaining
ch	chain stitch	rep	repeat(s)
ch-	refers to chain or space previously made. For example ch-1 space.	rnd(s)	round(s)
CL	cluster	RS	right side
dc	double crochet	sc	single crochet
dec	decrease	sc2tog	single crochet 2 together
dtr	double treble crochet	sk	skip
FL	front loop(s)	sl st	slip stitch
foll	follow, follows, following	sp(s)	space(s)
Fpdc	front post double crochet	st(s)	stitch(es)
hdc	half double crochet	tog	together
inc	increase	tr	treble crochet
lp(s)	loop(s)	WS	wrong side
		yo	yarn over

Crochet Terms

British vs American Crochet Terms			
\multicolumn{2}{c}{British English}		\multicolumn{2}{c}{US-American English}	
dc	double crochet	sc	single crochet
htr	half treble crochet	hdc	half double crochet
tr	treble	dc	double crochet
dtr	double treble	tr	treble
trtr	triple treble	dtr	double treble
	miss		skip
	tension		gauge
yoh	yarn over hook	yo	yarn over
All pattern instructions use US-American English terms			

Skill Level Definitions

Beginner / Débutant / Novicecia

A beginner project is for first-time crocheters using basic stitches. Beginner projects have minimal shaping.

Easy / Facile / Fácil

Easy projects use yarn with basic stitches, repetitive stitch patterns, simple color changes, with simple shaping and finishing.

Intermediate / Intermédiaire / Intermedio

Intermediate projects use a variety of techniques, such as basic lace patterns or color patterns. This level has mid-level shaping and finishing.

Experienced / Experimenté / Experiencia

Projects for experienced crocheters have intricate stitch patterns, techniques and dimension, such as non-repeating patterns, multi-color techniques, fine threads, small hooks, detailed shaping and refined finishing.

*Skill level and yarn weight graphics are provided by http://www.yarnstandards.com

Special Stitches

Front Post and Back Post Double Crochet

The front post and back post double crochet stitches or Fpdc and Bpdc are use to make raised textural crochet. Half double crochet can also be used and the abbreviation is Fphdc or Bphdc.

Fpdc-*Front Post Double Crochet*

Yarn over, insert hook from front to back to front around post of the corresponding stitch below, yarn over and pull up a loop, yarn over, draw through 2 loops on hook, yarn over, and draw through last 2 loops.

Bpdc – *Back Post Double Crochet*

Yarn over, insert hook from back to front to back around post of the corresponding stitch below, yarn over and pull up a loop, yarn over, draw through 2 loops on hook, yarn over, and draw through last 2 loops.

Loop Stitch

The loop stitch is worked from a wrong side row of your project. To make a loop stitch, insert your hook into the next stitch, just as you would for a single crochet. Wrap the yarn from front to back over the index finger of the hand holding the yarn. I usually just put my index finger under my working yarn and lift up to make the loop. Place your hook behind both ends of the loop and catch them with your hook.

Pull both strands through the stitch on your hook. There are now three strands of yarn on your hook.

Drop the loop and pick up your working yarn, wrap the yarn over your hook and pull through all three loops on the hook to finish the stitch.

Single Crochet 2 Together

Single crochet 2 together or sc2tog is a technique use to decrease stitches.

To single crochet 2 stitches together insert hook into the next stitch, yarn over, and pull up a loop. Insert hook into next stitch, yarn over, and pull up a loop. Yarn over, draw through all 3 loops on hook. You have now decreased one stitch.

Pretty in Pink

Quick and easy slipper boots that can be done all in one color or make the cuff and slipper in two colors. The slippers in the photo were crocheted using Loops & Threads Charisma bulky weight yarn in Fuchsia, Think Pink, and White.

Instructions

Easy / Facile / Fácil

Finished Sizes

Instructions given fit ladies and children's shoe sizes X-small with changes for small, medium, and large in parenthesis. The sizes are color coded for easier reading.

Finished Measurements

Adult - X-Small (3-4) 8 1/2" Small (5-6) 9" Medium (7-8) 9 1/2" Large (9-10) 10"

Children - X-Small (7-8) 6" Small (9-10) 6 1/2" Medium (11-12) 7" Large (1-2) 8"

Materials

Loops & Threads Charisma bulky weight acrylic yarn or any bulky weight yarn. (3.5 oz. / 109 yds / 100g per skein).

Note: Yarn amounts are to make 2 slippers using one color.

Adult - X-Small - 4.5 oz. / 128g Small - 5.0 oz. / 142g Medium - 6.5 oz. / 184g Large - 8 oz. / 227g

Children - X-Small - 2 oz. / 57g Small - 2.5 oz. / 71g Medium - 4 oz. / 113g Large - 4.5 oz. / 128g

Notions

Tapestry or yarn needle

Stitch markers

Hook

Size L (8.0 mm) crochet hook or size to obtain gauge.

Gauge

5 sc = 2 inches; 6 sc rows = 2 inches

SPECIAL STITCHES

Single crochet 2 together (sc2tog): Sc2tog means to use single crochet to join two stitches together or decrease by one stitch.

Insert the hook into a stitch and draw up a loop. Insert the hook into the next stitch and draw up a loop. Yarn over, draw through all 3 loops on hook.

PATTERN NOTES

Instructions for the cuff and foot of the slipper boots are written separately so you can make each section a different color if you wish.

Stitch markers are used to mark the center stitch of the foot rows. To place a marker (PM) first crochet the number of stitches indicated in the pattern, place marker (PM) on the last stitch crocheted, then finish the row as directed. For the following rows move the marker by crocheting up to the stitch just before the marker, remove the marker, crochet the stitch, and then replace the marker.

In addition to size information being in parenthesis they are color coded to make the patterns easier to read. Numbers and letters in black are for all sizes.

Adult

X-Small   Small   Medium   Large

Children

X-Small   Small   Medium   Large

On last row of cuff change to foot color if desired. To change colors in single crochet, pull up a loop in the current color you are using, draw the new color through the last two loops on the hook to complete the single crochet stitch.

SLIPPER BOOTS (Make 2)

CUFF (Adult)

Row 1: Ch 22 (24, 26, 28). Sc in 2nd ch from hook and in each rem ch across. Ch 1. Turn. 21 (23, 25, 27) sts.

Rows 2-10: Sc in each st across. Ch 1. Turn. 21 (23, 25, 27) sts.

CUFF (Children)

Row 1: Ch 18 (18, 20, 22). Sc in 2nd ch from hook and in each rem ch across. Ch 1. Turn. 17 (17, 19, 21) sts.

Rows 2-6 (6, 8, 8): Sc in each st across. Ch 1. Turn. 17 (17, 19, 21) sts.

FOOT (Adult)

Rows 1-2: Sc in first 11 (12, 13, 14) sts, place marker for center st, sc in rem sts. Ch 1. Turn. 21 (23, 25, 27) sts.

Row 3: Sc in each st to within 2 sts of marker, 2 dc in each of the next 2 sts, 5 dc in center st (placing the marker in the 3rd dc), 2 dc in each of next 2 sts, sc in each rem st to end of row. Ch 1. Turn. 29 (31, 33, 35) sts.

Row 4: Sc in each st across. Ch 1. Turn. 29 (31, 33, 35) sts.

Row 5: Rep Row 3. Ch 1. Turn. 37 (39, 41, 43) sts.

Row 6: Sc in each st across. Ch 1. Turn. 37 (39, 41, 43) sts.

Row 7: Rep Row 3. Ch 1. Turn. 45 (47, 49, 51) sts.

Rows 8-8 (9,10, 11): Rep row 4. Ch 1. Turn. 45 (47, 49, 51) sts.

Rows 9-10 (10-11, 11-12, 12-13): Sc in each st to within 2 sts of marker, sc2tog, sc in center st, sc2tog, sc in each rem st to end of row. Ch 1. Turn. 41 (43, 45, 47) sts.

Row 11 (12, 13, 14): Sc2tog, sc in each st to within 2 sts of marker, sc2tog, sc in center st, sc2 tog, sc in each rem st up to last 2 sts, sc2tog. Ch 1. Turn. 37 (39, 41, 43) sts.

Row 12 (13, 14, 15): Sc2tog, sc in each st to within 4 sts of marker, sc2tog 2 times, sc in center st, sc2 tog 2 times, sc in each rem st up to last 2 sts, sc2tog. Fasten off. 31 (33, 35, 37) sts.

Finishing

Weave in all loose ends. Whip stitch center back and foot seam with matching yarn.

FOOT (Children)

Row 1-2: Sc in first 9 (9, 10, 11) sts, place marker for center st, sc in rem sts. Ch 1. Turn. 17 (17, 19, 21) sts.

Row 3: 2 sc in first st. Sc in each st to within 1 st of marker, 2 dc in the next st, 5 dc in center st (placing the marker in the 3rd dc), 2 dc in the next st, sc in each rem st to end of row with 2 sc in last st. Ch 1. Turn. 25 (25, 27, 29) sts.

Row 4: Sc in each st across. Ch 1. Turn. 25 (25, 27, 29) sts.

Row 5: (For X-Small **and** Medium**)** Sc in each st to within 1 st of marker, 2 dc in the next st, 5 dc in center st (placing the marker in the 3rd dc), 2 dc in the next st, sc in each rem st to end of row. Ch 1. Turn. 31 (33) sts.

Row 5: (For Small **and** Large**)** 2 sc in first st. Sc in each st to within 1 st of marker, 2 dc in the next st, 5 dc in center st (placing the marker in the 3rd dc), 2 dc in the next st, sc in each rem st to end of row with 2 sc in last st. Ch 1. Turn. 33 (37) sts.

Row 6: Sc in each st across. Ch 1. Turn. 31 (33, 33, 37) sts.

Row 7: (For X-Small **and** Small**)** Sc in each st to within 2 sts of marker, sc2tog, sc in center st, sc2tog, sc in each rem st to end of row. Ch 1. Turn. 29 (31) sts.

Row 7: (For Medium **and** Large**)** Sc in each st to within 1 st of marker, 2 dc in the next st, 5 dc in center st (placing the marker in the 3rd dc), 2 dc in the next st, sc in each rem st to end of row. Ch 1. Turn. 39 (43) sts.

Row 8: (For X-Small**)** Sc2tog, sc in each st to within 2 sts of marker, sc2tog, sc in center st, sc2tog, sc in each rem st to end of row. Ch 1. Turn. 25 sts.

Row 8: (For Small**)** Sc in each st to within 2 sts of marker, sc2tog, sc in center st, sc2tog, sc in each rem st to end of row. Ch 1. Turn. 29 sts.

Row 8: (For Medium**)** Sc in each st across. Ch 1. Turn. 39 sts.

Row 8: (For Large**)** Sc in each st across. Ch 1. Turn. 43 sts.

Row 9: (For X-Small**)** Sc2tog, sc in each st to within 4 sts of marker, sc2tog 2 times, sc in center st, sc2 tog 2 times, sc in each rem st up to last 2 sts, sc2tog. Fasten off. 19 sts.

Row 9: (For Small**)** Sc2tog, sc in each st to within 2 sts of marker, sc2tog, sc in center st, sc2tog, sc in each rem st to end of row. Ch 1. Turn. 25 sts.

Row 9: (For Medium**)** Sc in each st to within 2 sts of marker, sc2tog, sc in center st, sc2tog, sc in each rem st to end of row. Ch 1. Turn. (37) sts.

Row 9: (For Large**)** Sc in each st across. Ch 1. Turn. 43 sts.

Row 10: (For Small**)** Sc2tog, sc in each st to within 4 sts of marker, sc2tog 2 times, sc in center st, sc2 tog 2 times, sc in each rem st up to last 2 sts, sc2tog. Fasten off. 19 sts.

Row 10: (For Medium**)** Sc2tog, sc in each st to within 2 sts of marker, sc2tog, sc in center st, sc2tog, sc in each rem st to end of row. Ch 1. Turn. 33 sts.

Row 10: (For Large**)** Sc in each st to within 2 sts of marker, sc2tog, sc in center st, sc2tog, sc in each rem st to end of row. Ch 1. Turn. 41 sts.

Row 11: (For Medium **and** Large**)** Sc2tog, sc in each st to within 2 sts of marker, sc2tog, sc in center st, sc2tog, sc in each rem st to end of row. Ch 1. Turn. 29 (37) sts.

Row 12: (For Medium**)** Sc2tog, sc in each st to within 4 sts of marker, sc2tog 2 times, sc in center st, sc2 tog 2 times, sc in each rem st up to last 2 sts, sc2tog. Fasten off. 23 sts.

Row 12: (For Large**)** Sc2tog, sc in each st to within 2 sts of marker, sc2tog, sc in center st, sc2tog, sc in each rem st to end of row. Ch 1. Turn. 33 sts.

Row 13: (For Large**)** Sc2tog, sc in each st to within 4 sts of marker, sc2tog 2 times, sc in center st, sc2 tog 2 times, sc in each rem st up to last 2 sts, sc2tog. Fasten off. 27 sts.

Finishing

Weave in all loose ends. Whip stitch center back and foot seam with matching yarn.

Boots With The Fur

These slipper boots are a lot of fun and can be made all in one color or make the cuff and slipper in two colors. The slippers in the photo were crocheted using Debra Norville Serenity Chunky yarn in White, Grape Jam, and Seven Seas.

Instructions

Easy / Facile / Fácil

Finished Sizes

Instructions given fit ladies and children's shoe sizes X-small with changes for small, medium, and large in parenthesis. The sizes are color coded for easier reading.

Finished Measurements

Adult - X-Small (3-4) 8 1/2" Small (5-6) 9" Medium (7-8) 9 1/2" Large (9-10) 10"

Children - X-Small (7-8) 6" Small (9-10) 6 1/2" Medium (11-12) 7" Large (1-2) 8"

Materials

 Debra Norville Serenity Chunky Yarn or any bulky weight yarn. (3.5 oz. / 109 yds / 100g per skein).

Main Color (MC)

Adult - X-Small - 3 oz. / 85g Small - 3.5 oz. / 100g Medium - 3.5 oz. / 100g Large - 5 oz. / 142g

Children - X-Small - 1.5 oz. / 43g Small - 2 oz. / 57g Medium - 2.5 oz. / 71g Large - 3 oz. / 85g

Contrasting Color (CC)

Adult - X-Small - 3 oz. / 85g Small - 3.5 oz. / 100g Medium - 4.0 oz. / 113g Large - 4.5 oz. / 128g

Children - X-Small - 1.5 oz. / 43g Small - 2 oz. / 57g Medium - 2 oz. / 57g Large - 2.5 oz. / 71g

Notions

Tapestry or yarn needle

Stitch markers

Hook

Size L (8.0 mm) crochet hook or size to obtain gauge.

Gauge

5 sc = 2 inches; 6 sc rows = 2 inches

SPECIAL STITCHES

Single crochet 2 together (sc2tog): Sc2tog means to use single crochet to join two stitches together or decrease by one stitch.

Insert the hook into a stitch and draw up a loop. Insert the hook into the next stitch and draw up a loop. Yarn over, draw through all 3 loops on hook.

Loop Stitch: The loop stitch is worked from a wrong side row of your project. To make a loop stitch, insert your hook into the next stitch, just as you would for a single crochet. Wrap the yarn from front to back over the index finger of the hand holding the yarn. I usually just put my index finger under my working yarn and lift up to make the loop. Place your hook behind both ends of the loop and catch them with your hook. Pull both strands through the stitch on your hook. There are now three strands of yarn on your hook. Drop the loop and pick up your working yarn, wrap the yarn over your hook and pull through all three loops on the hook to finish the stitch.

PATTERN NOTES

Instructions for the cuff and foot of the slipper boots are written separately so you can make each section a different color if you wish.

Stitch markers are used to mark the center stitch of the foot rows. To place a marker (PM) first crochet the number of stitches indicated in the pattern, place marker (PM) on the last stitch crocheted, then finish the row as directed. For the following rows move the marker by crocheting up to the stitch just before the marker, remove the marker, crochet the stitch, and then replace the marker.

On last row of cuff change to MC. To change colors in loop stitch, pull up a loop in the current color you are using, draw the new color through the three loops on the hook to complete the loop stitch.

In addition to size information being in parenthesis they are color coded to make the patterns easier to read. Numbers and letters in black are for all sizes.

Adult

X-Small   Small   Medium   Large

Children

X-Small   Small   Medium   Large

SLIPPER BOOTS (Make 2)

CUFF (Adult)

Row 1: With CC, ch 22 (24, 26, 28). Sc in 2nd ch from hook and in each rem ch across. Ch 1. Turn. 21 (23, 25, 27) sts.

Row 2: Loop st in each st across. Ch 1. Turn. 21 (23, 25, 27) sts.

Row 3: Sc in each st across. Ch 1. Turn. 21 (23, 25, 27) sts.

Rows 4-12: Rep rows 2-3. Ch 1. Turn. 21 (23, 25, 27) sts. On the last stitch of the last row change to MC.

CUFF (Children)

Row 1: With CC, ch 18 (18, 20, 22). Sc in 2nd ch from hook and in each rem ch across. Ch 1. Turn. 17 (17, 19, 21) sts.

Row 2: Loop st in each st across. Ch 1. Turn. 17 (17, 19, 21) sts.

Row 3: Sc in each st across. Ch 1. Turn. 17 (17, 19, 21) sts.

Rows 4-6 (6, 8, 8): Rep rows 2-3. Ch 1. Turn. 17 (17, 19, 21) sts. On the last stitch of the last row change to MC.

FOOT (Adult)

Rows 1-2: With MC, sc in first 11 (12, 13, 14) sts, place marker for center st, sc in rem sts. Ch 1. Turn. 21 (23, 25, 27) sts.

Row 3: Sc in each st to within 2 sts of marker, 2 dc in each of the next 2 sts, 5 dc in center st (placing the marker in the 3rd dc), 2 dc in each of next 2 sts, sc in each rem st to end of row. Ch 1. Turn. 29 (31, 33, 35) sts.

Row 4: Sc in each st across. Ch 1. Turn. 29 (31, 33, 35) sts.

Row 5: Rep Row 3. Ch 1. Turn. 37 (39, 41, 43) sts.

Row 6: Sc in each st across. Ch 1. Turn. 37 (39, 41, 43) sts.

Row 7: Rep Row 3. Ch 1. Turn. 45 (47, 49, 51) sts.

Rows 8-8 (9,10, 11): Rep row 4. Ch 1. Turn. 45 (47, 49, 51) sts.

Rows 9-10 (10-11, 11-12, 12-13): Sc in each st to within 2 sts of marker, sc2tog, sc in center st, sc2tog, sc in each rem st to end of row. Ch 1. Turn. 41 (43, 45, 47) sts.

Row 11 (12, 13, 14): Sc2tog, sc in each st to within 2 sts of marker, sc2tog, sc in center st, sc2 tog, sc in each rem st up to last 2 sts, sc2tog. Ch 1. Turn. 37 (39, 41, 43) sts.

Row 12 (13, 14, 15): Sc2tog, sc in each st to within 4 sts of marker, sc2tog 2 times, sc in center st, sc2 tog 2 times, sc in each rem st up to last 2 sts, sc2tog. Fasten off. 31 (33, 35, 37) sts.

Finishing

Weave in all loose ends. Whip stitch center back and foot seam with matching yarn.

FOOT (Children)

Row 1-2: With MC, sc in first 9 (9, 10, 11) sts, place marker for center st, sc in rem sts. Ch 1. Turn. 17 (17, 19, 21) sts.

Row 3: 2 sc in first st. Sc in each st to within 1 st of marker, 2 dc in the next st, 5 dc in center st (placing the marker in the 3rd dc), 2 dc in the next st, sc in each rem st to end of row with 2 sc in last st. Ch 1. Turn. 25 (25, 27, 29) sts.

Row 4: Sc in each st across. Ch 1. Turn. 25 (25, 27, 29) sts.

Row 5: (For X-Small and Medium) Sc in each st to within 1 st of marker, 2 dc in the next st, 5 dc in center st (placing the marker in the 3rd dc), 2 dc in the next st, sc in each rem st to end of row. Ch 1. Turn. 31 (33) sts.

Row 5: (For Small and Large) 2 sc in first st. Sc in each st to within 1 st of marker, 2 dc in the next st, 5 dc in center st (placing the marker in the 3rd dc), 2 dc in the next st, sc in each rem st to end of row with 2 sc in last st. Ch 1. Turn. 33 (37) sts.

Row 6: Sc in each st across. Ch 1. Turn. 31 (33, 33, 37) sts.

Row 7: (For X-Small and Small) Sc in each st to within 2 sts of marker, sc2tog, sc in center st, sc2tog, sc in each rem st to end of row. Ch 1. Turn. 29 (31) sts.

Row 7: (For Medium and Large) Sc in each st to within 1 st of marker, 2 dc in the next st, 5 dc in center st (placing the marker in the 3rd dc), 2 dc in the next st, sc in each rem st to end of row. Ch 1. Turn. 39 (43) sts.

Row 8: (For X-Small) Sc2tog, sc in each st to within 2 sts of marker, sc2tog, sc in center st, sc2tog, sc in each rem st to end of row. Ch 1. Turn. 25 sts.

Row 8: (For Small) Sc in each st to within 2 sts of marker, sc2tog, sc in center st, sc2tog, sc in each rem st to end of row. Ch 1. Turn. 29 sts.

Row 8: (For Medium) Sc in each st across. Ch 1. Turn. 39 sts.

Row 8: (For Large) Sc in each st across. Ch 1. Turn. 43 sts.

Row 9: (For X-Small) Sc2tog, sc in each st to within 4 sts of marker, sc2tog 2 times, sc in center st, sc2 tog 2 times, sc in each rem st up to last 2 sts, sc2tog. Fasten off. 19 sts.

Row 9: (For Small) Sc2tog, sc in each st to within 2 sts of marker, sc2tog, sc in center st, sc2tog, sc in each rem st to end of row. Ch 1. Turn. 25 sts.

Row 9: (For Medium) Sc in each st to within 2 sts of marker, sc2tog, sc in center st, sc2tog, sc in each rem st to end of row. Ch 1. Turn. (37) sts.

Row 9: (For Large) Sc in each st across. Ch 1. Turn. 43 sts.

Row 10: (For Small) Sc2tog, sc in each st to within 4 sts of marker, sc2tog 2 times, sc in center st, sc2 tog 2 times, sc in each rem st up to last 2 sts, sc2tog. Fasten off. 19 sts.

Row 10: (For Medium) Sc2tog, sc in each st to within 2 sts of marker, sc2tog, sc in center st, sc2tog, sc in each rem st to end of row. Ch 1. Turn. 33 sts.

Row 10: (For Large) Sc in each st to within 2 sts of marker, sc2tog, sc in center st, sc2tog, sc in each rem st to end of row. Ch 1. Turn. 41 sts.

Row 11: (For Medium and Large) Sc2tog, sc in each st to within 2 sts of marker, sc2tog, sc in center st, sc2tog, sc in each rem st to end of row. Ch 1. Turn. 29 (37) sts.

Row 12: (For Medium) Sc2tog, sc in each st to within 4 sts of marker, sc2tog 2 times, sc in center st, sc2 tog 2 times, sc in each rem st up to last 2 sts, sc2tog. Fasten off. 23 sts.

Row 12: (For Large) Sc2tog, sc in each st to within 2 sts of marker, sc2tog, sc in center st, sc2tog, sc in each rem st to end of row. Ch 1. Turn. 33 sts.

Row 13: (For Large) Sc2tog, sc in each st to within 4 sts of marker, sc2tog 2 times, sc in center st, sc2 tog 2 times, sc in each rem st up to last 2 sts, sc2tog. Fasten off. 27 sts.

Finishing

Weave in all loose ends. Whip stitch center back and foot seam with matching yarn.

Ribbed Lounging Boots

The slippers in the photo were crocheted using Loops & Threads Charisma bulky weight yarn in Ash and Sunny Day.

Instructions

Easy / Facile / Fácil

Finished Sizes

Instructions given fit ladies and children's shoe sizes X-small with changes for small, medium, and large in parenthesis. The sizes are color coded for easier reading.

Finished Measurements

Adult - X-Small (3-4) 8 1/2" Small (5-6) 9" Medium (7-8) 9 1/2" Large (9-10) 10"

Children - X-Small (7-8) 6" Small (9-10) 6 1/2" Medium (11-12) 7" Large (1-2) 8"

Materials

[5 BULKY] Loops & Threads Charisma bulky weight acrylic yarn or any bulky weight yarn. (3.5 oz. / 109 yds / 100g per skein).

Note: Yarn amounts are to make 2 slippers using one color.

Adult - X-Small - 4.5 oz. / 128g Small - 5 oz. / 142g Medium - 6.5 oz. / 184g Large - 8 oz. / 227g

Children - X-Small - 2 oz. / 57g Small - 2.5 oz. / 71g Medium - 4 oz. / 113g Large - 4.5 oz. / 128g

Notions

Tapestry or yarn needle

Stitch markers

Hook

Size L (8.0 mm) crochet hook or size to obtain gauge.

Gauge

5 sc = 2 inches; 6 sc rows = 2 inches

SPECIAL STITCHES

Single crochet 2 together (sc2tog): Sc2tog means to use single crochet to join two stitches together or decrease by one stitch.

Insert the hook into a stitch and draw up a loop. Insert the hook into the next stitch and draw up a loop. Yarn over, draw through all 3 loops on hook.

Front Post and Back Post Double Crochet

The front post and back post double crochet stitches or Fpdc and Bpdc are use to make raised textural crochet. Half double crochet can also be used and the abbreviation is Fphdc or Bphdc.

Fpdc-*Front Post Double Crochet*

Yarn over, insert hook from front to back to front around post of the corresponding stitch below, yarn over and pull up a loop, yarn over, draw through 2 loops on hook, yarn over, and draw through last 2 loops.

Bpdc - *Front Post Double Crochet*

Yarn over, insert hook from back to front to back around post of the corresponding stitch below, yarn over and pull up a loop, yarn over, draw through 2 loops on hook, yarn over, and draw through last 2 loops.

PATTERN NOTES

Instructions for the cuff and foot of the slipper boots are written separately so you can make each section a different color if you wish.

Stitch markers are used to mark the center stitch of the foot rows. To place a marker (PM) first crochet the number of stitches indicated in the pattern, place marker (PM) on the last stitch crocheted, then finish the row as directed. For the following rows move the marker by crocheting up to the stitch just before the marker, remove the marker, crochet the stitch, and then replace the marker.

In addition to size information being in parenthesis they are color coded to make the patterns easier to read. Numbers and letters in black are for all sizes.

Adult

X-Small   Small   Medium   Large

Children

X-Small   Small   Medium   Large

On last row of cuff change to the foot color if desired. To change colors in half double crochet, yo, pull up a loop in the current color you are using, draw the new color through three loops on the hook to complete the single crochet stitch.

SLIPPER BOOTS (Make 2)

CUFF (Adult)

Row 1: Ch 23 (25, 27, 29). Hdc in 3rd ch from hook, hdc in each ch across. Ch 2. Turn. 21 (23, 25, 27) sts.

Rows 2: Fphdc around 2nd hdc from previous row *(hdc directly below turning ch is the 1st hdc),**Bphdc around next hdc from previous row, Fphdc around next hdc from previous row, rep from * across row ending hdc in turning ch. Ch 2. Turn. 21 (23, 25, 27) sts.

Rows 3-12: *Fphdc around Fphdc from previous row, Bphdc around Bphdc from previous row, rep from * across row ending hdc in turning ch. Ch 2. Turn. 21 (23, 25, 27) sts.

CUFF (Children)

Row 1: Ch 19 (19, 21, 23). Hdc in 3rd ch from hook, hdc in each ch across. Ch 2. Turn. 17 (17, 19, 21) sts.

Rows 2: Fphdc around 2nd hdc from previous row *(hdc directly below turning ch is the 1st hdc),**Bphdc around next hdc from previous row, Fphdc around next hdc from previous row, rep from * across row ending hdc in turning ch. Ch 2. Turn. 17 (17, 19, 21) sts.

Rows 3-4 (4, 6, 6): *Fphdc around Fphdc from previous row, Bphdc around Bphdc from previous row, rep from * across row ending hdc in turning ch. Ch 2. Turn. 17 (17, 19, 21) sts.

FOOT (Adult)

Rows 1-2: Sc in first 11 (12, 13, 14) sts, place marker for center st, sc in rem sts. Ch 1. Turn. 21 (23, 25, 27) sts.

Row 3: Sc in each st to within 2 sts of marker, 2 dc in each of the next 2 sts, 5 dc in center st (placing the marker in the 3rd dc), 2 dc in each of next 2 sts, sc in each rem st to end of row. Ch 1. Turn. 29 (31, 33, 35) sts.

Row 4: Sc in each st across. Ch 1. Turn. 29 (31, 33, 35) sts.

Row 5: Rep Row 3. Ch 1. Turn. 37 (39, 41, 43) sts.

Row 6: Sc in each st across. Ch 1. Turn. 37 (39, 41, 43) sts.

Row 7: Rep Row 3. Ch 1. Turn. 45 (47, 49, 51) sts.

Rows 8-8 (9, 10, 11): Rep row 4. Ch 1. Turn. 45 (47, 49, 51) sts.

Rows 9-10 (10-11, 11-12, 12-13): Sc in each st to within 2 sts of marker, sc2tog, sc in center st, sc2tog, sc in each rem st to end of row. Ch 1. Turn. 41 (43, 45, 47) sts.

Row 11 (12, 13, 14): Sc2tog, sc in each st to within 2 sts of marker, sc2tog, sc in center st, sc2 tog, sc in each rem st up to last 2 sts, sc2tog. Ch 1. Turn. 37 (39, 41, 43) sts.

Row 12 (13, 14, 15): Sc2tog, sc in each st to within 4 sts of marker, sc2tog 2 times, sc in center st, sc2 tog 2 times, sc in each rem st up to last 2 sts, sc2tog. Fasten off. 31 (33, 35, 37) sts.

Finishing

Weave in all loose ends. Whip stitch center back and foot seam with matching yarn.

FOOT (Children)

Row 1-2: Sc in first 9 (9, 10, 11) sts, place marker for center st, sc in rem sts. Ch 1. Turn. 17 (17, 19, 21) sts.

Row 3: 2 sc in first st. Sc in each st to within 1 st of marker, 2 dc in the next st, 5 dc in center st (placing the marker in the 3rd dc), 2 dc in the next st, sc in each rem st to end of row with 2 sc in last st. Ch 1. Turn. 25 (25, 27, 29) sts.

Row 4: Sc in each st across. Ch 1. Turn. 25 (25, 27, 29) sts.

Row 5: (For X-Small and Medium) Sc in each st to within 1 st of marker, 2 dc in the next st, 5 dc in center st (placing the marker in the 3rd dc), 2 dc in the next st, sc in each rem st to end of row. Ch 1. Turn. 31 (33) sts.

Row 5: (For Small and Large) 2 sc in first st. Sc in each st to within 1 st of marker, 2 dc in the next st, 5 dc in center st (placing the marker in the 3rd dc), 2 dc in the next st, sc in each rem st to end of row with 2 sc in last st. Ch 1. Turn. 33 (37) sts.

Row 6: Sc in each st across. Ch 1. Turn. 31 (33, 33, 37) sts.

Row 7: (For X-Small and Small) Sc in each st to within 2 sts of marker, sc2tog, sc in center st, sc2tog, sc in each rem st to end of row. Ch 1. Turn. 29 (31) sts.

Row 7: (For Medium and Large) Sc in each st to within 1 st of marker, 2 dc in the next st, 5 dc in center st (placing the marker in the 3rd dc), 2 dc in the next st, sc in each rem st to end of row. Ch 1. Turn. 39 (43) sts.

Row 8: (For X-Small) Sc2tog, sc in each st to within 2 sts of marker, sc2tog, sc in center st, sc2tog, sc in each rem st to end of row. Ch 1. Turn. 25 sts.

Row 8: (For Small) Sc in each st to within 2 sts of marker, sc2tog, sc in center st, sc2tog, sc in each rem st to end of row. Ch 1. Turn. 29 sts.

Row 8: (For Medium) Sc in each st across. Ch 1. Turn. 39 sts.

Row 8: (For Large) Sc in each st across. Ch 1. Turn. 43 sts.

Row 9: (For X-Small) Sc2tog, sc in each st to within 4 sts of marker, sc2tog 2 times, sc in center st, sc2 tog 2 times, sc in each rem st up to last 2 sts, sc2tog. Fasten off. 19 sts.

Row 9: (For Small) Sc2tog, sc in each st to within 2 sts of marker, sc2tog, sc in center st, sc2tog, sc in each rem st to end of row. Ch 1. Turn. 25 sts.

Row 9: (For Medium) Sc in each st to within 2 sts of marker, sc2tog, sc in center st, sc2tog, sc in each rem st to end of row. Ch 1. Turn. **(37)** sts.

Row 9: (For Large) Sc in each st across. Ch 1. Turn. 43 sts.

Row 10: (For Small) Sc2tog, sc in each st to within 4 sts of marker, sc2tog 2 times, sc in center st, sc2 tog 2 times, sc in each rem st up to last 2 sts, sc2tog. Fasten off. 19 sts.

Row 10: (For Medium) Sc2tog, sc in each st to within 2 sts of marker, sc2tog, sc in center st, sc2tog, sc in each rem st to end of row. Ch 1. Turn. 33 sts.

Row 10: (For Large) Sc in each st to within 2 sts of marker, sc2tog, sc in center st, sc2tog, sc in each rem st to end of row. Ch 1. Turn. 41 sts.

Row 11: (For Medium and Large) Sc2tog, sc in each st to within 2 sts of marker, sc2tog, sc in center st, sc2tog, sc in each rem st to end of row. Ch 1. Turn. 29 **(37)** sts.

Row 12: (For Medium) Sc2tog, sc in each st to within 4 sts of marker, sc2tog 2 times, sc in center st, sc2 tog 2 times, sc in each rem st up to last 2 sts, sc2tog. Fasten off. 23 sts.

Row 12: (For Large) Sc2tog, sc in each st to within 2 sts of marker, sc2tog, sc in center st, sc2tog, sc in each rem st to end of row. Ch 1. Turn. 33 sts.

Row 13: (For Large) Sc2tog, sc in each st to within 4 sts of marker, sc2tog 2 times, sc in center st, sc2 tog 2 times, sc in each rem st up to last 2 sts, sc2tog. Fasten off. 27 sts.

Finishing

Weave in all loose ends. Whip stitch center back and foot seam with matching yarn.

Cozy Bobble Boots

Warm and cozy bobble boots! The slippers in the photo were crocheted using Loops & Threads Charisma bulky weight yarn in Chocolate Cupcake and Lakeside.

Instructions

Easy / Facile / Fácil

Finished Sizes

Instructions given fit ladies and children's shoe sizes x-small with changes for small, medium, and large in parenthesis. The sizes are color coded for easier reading.

Finished Measurements

Adult - X-Small (3-4) 8 1/2" Small (5-6) 9" Medium (7-8) 9 1/2" Large (9-10) 10"

Children - X-Small (7-8) 6" Small (9-10) 6 1/2" Medium (11-12) 7" Large (1-2) 8"

Materials

Loops & Threads Charisma bulky weight acrylic yarn or any bulky weight yarn. (3.5 oz. / 109 yds / 100g per skein).

Note: Yarn amounts are to make 2 slippers using one color.

Adult - X-Small - 4.5 oz. / 128g Small - 5 oz. / 142g Medium - 6.5 oz. / 184g Large - 8 oz. / 227g

Children - X-Small - 2 oz. / 57g Small - 2.5 oz. / 71g Medium - 4 oz. / 113g Large - 4.5 oz. / 128g

Notions

Tapestry or yarn needle

Stitch markers

Hook

Size L (8.0 mm) crochet hook or size to obtain gauge.

Gauge

5 sc = 2 inches; 6 sc rows = 2 inches

SPECIAL STITCHES

Single crochet 2 together (sc2tog): Sc2tog means to use single crochet to join two stitches together or decrease by one stitch.

Insert the hook into a stitch and draw up a loop. Insert the hook into the next stitch and draw up a loop. Yarn over, draw through all 3 loops on hook.

PATTERN NOTES

Instructions for the cuff and foot of the slipper boots are written separately so you can make each section a different color if you wish.

Stitch markers are used to mark the center stitch of the foot rows. To place a marker (PM) first crochet the number of stitches indicated in the pattern, place marker (PM) on the last stitch crocheted, then finish the row as directed. For the following rows move the marker by crocheting up to the stitch just before the marker, remove the marker, crochet the stitch, and then replace the marker.

In addition to size information being in parenthesis they are color coded to make the patterns easier to read. Numbers and letters in black are for all sizes.

Adult

X-Small   Small   Medium   Large

Children

X-Small   Small   Medium   Large

On last row of cuff change to foot color if desired. To change colors in single crochet, pull up a loop in the current color you are using, draw the new color through the last two loops on the hook to complete the single crochet stitch.

SLIPPER BOOTS (Make 2)

CUFF (Adult)

Row 1: Ch 23 (25, 27, 29). Sc in 2nd ch from hook, sc in each ch across. Ch 1. Turn. 22 (24, 26, 28) sts.

Rows 2: *Sc in first st, tr in next st, rep from * across row ending sc in last 2 sts. Ch 1. Turn. 22 (24, 26, 28) sts.

Row 3: Sc in each st across row. Ch 1. Turn. 22 (24, 26, 28) sts.

Row 4: Sc in first 2 sc, *tr in next st, sc in next st, rep from * across row ending sc in last st. Ch 1. Turn. 22 (24, 26, 28) sts.

Row 5: Sc in each st across row. Ch 1. Turn. 22 (24, 26, 28) sts.

Rows 6-12: Rep rows 2-5. 22 (24, 26, 28) sts.

CUFF (Children)

Row 1: Ch 19 (19, 21, 23). Sc in 2nd ch from hook, sc in each ch across. Ch 1. Turn. 18 (18, 20, 22) sts.

Rows 2: *Sc in first st, tr in next st, rep from * across row ending sc in last 2 sts. Ch 1. Turn. 18 (18, 20, 22) sts.

Row 3: Sc in each st across row. Ch 1. Turn. 18 (18, 20, 22) sts.

Row 4: Sc in first 2 sc, *tr in next st, sc in next st, rep from * across row ending sc in last st. Ch 1. Turn. 18 (18, 20, 22) sts.

Row 5: Sc in each st across row. Ch 1. Turn. 18 (18, 20, 22) sts.

Rows 5-6 (6, 8, 8): Rep rows 2-5. 18 (18, 20, 22) sts.

FOOT (Adult)

Row 1: Sc in first 10 (11, 12, 13) sts, sc2tog, place marker for center st, sc in rem sts. Ch 1. Turn. 21 (23, 25, 27) sts.

Row 2: Sc in each st across. Ch 1. Turn. 21 (23, 25, 27) sts.

Row 3: Sc in each st to within 2 sts of marker, 2 dc in each of the next 2 sts, 5 dc in center st (placing the marker in the 3rd dc), 2 dc in each of next 2 sts, sc in each rem st to end of row. Ch 1. Turn. 29 (31, 33, 35) sts.

Row 4: Sc in each st across. Ch 1. Turn. 29 (31, 33, 35) sts.

Row 5: Rep Row 3. Ch 1. Turn. 37 (39, 41, 43) sts.

Row 6: Sc in each st across. Ch 1. Turn. 37 (39, 41, 43) sts.

Row 7: Rep Row 3. Ch 1. Turn. 45 (47, 49, 51) sts.

Rows 8-8 (9, 10, 11): Rep row 4. Ch 1. Turn. 45 (47, 49, 51) sts.

Rows 9-10 (10-11, 11-12, 12-13): Sc in each st to within 2 sts of marker, sc2tog, sc in center st, sc2tog, sc in each rem st to end of row. Ch 1. Turn. 41 (43, 45, 47) sts.

Row 11 (12, 13, 14): Sc2tog, sc in each st to within 2 sts of marker, sc2tog, sc in center st, sc2 tog, sc in each rem st up to last 2 sts, sc2tog. Ch 1. Turn. 37 (39, 41, 43) sts.

Row 12 (13, 14, 15): Sc2tog, sc in each st to within 4 sts of marker, sc2tog 2 times, sc in center st, sc2 tog 2 times, sc in each rem st up to last 2 sts, sc2tog. Fasten off. 31 (33, 35, 37) sts.

Finishing

Weave in all loose ends. Whip stitch center back and foot seam with matching yarn.

FOOT (Children)

Row 1: Sc in first 8 (8, 9, 10) sts, sc2tog, place marker for center st, sc in rem sts. Ch 1. Turn. 17 (17, 19, 21) sts.

Row 2: Sc in each st across. Ch 1. Turn. 17 (17, 19, 21) sts.

Row 3: 2 sc in first st. Sc in each st to within 1 st of marker, 2 dc in the next st, 5 dc in center st (placing the marker in the 3rd dc), 2 dc in the next st, sc in each rem st to end of row with 2 sc in last st. Ch 1. Turn. 25 (25, 27, 29) sts.

Row 4: Sc in each st across. Ch 1. Turn. 25 (25, 27, 29) sts.

Row 5: (For X-Small and Medium) Sc in each st to within 1 st of marker, 2 dc in the next st, 5 dc in center st (placing the marker in the 3rd dc), 2 dc in the next st, sc in each rem st to end of row. Ch 1. Turn. 31 (33) sts.

Row 5: (For Small and Large) 2 sc in first st. Sc in each st to within 1 st of marker, 2 dc in the next st, 5 dc in center st (placing the marker in the 3rd dc), 2 dc in the next st, sc in each rem st to end of row with 2 sc in last st. Ch 1. Turn. 33 (37) sts.

Row 6: Sc in each st across. Ch 1. Turn. 31 (33, 33, 37) sts.

Row 7: (For X-Small and Small) Sc in each st to within 2 sts of marker, sc2tog, sc in center st, sc2tog, sc in each rem st to end of row. Ch 1. Turn. 29 (31) sts.

Row 7: (For Medium and Large) Sc in each st to within 1 st of marker, 2 dc in the next st, 5 dc in center st (placing the marker in the 3rd dc), 2 dc in the next st, sc in each rem st to end of row. Ch 1. Turn. 39 (43) sts.

Row 8: (For X-Small) Sc2tog, sc in each st to within 2 sts of marker, sc2tog, sc in center st, sc2tog, sc in each rem st to end of row. Ch 1. Turn. 25 sts.

Row 8: (For Small) Sc in each st to within 2 sts of marker, sc2tog, sc in center st, sc2tog, sc in each rem st to end of row. Ch 1. Turn. 29 sts.

Row 8: (For Medium) Sc in each st across. Ch 1. Turn. 39 sts.

Row 8: (For Large) Sc in each st across. Ch 1. Turn. 43 sts.

Row 9: (For X-Small) Sc2tog, sc in each st to within 4 sts of marker, sc2tog 2 times, sc in center st, sc2 tog 2 times, sc in each rem st up to last 2 sts, sc2tog. Fasten off. 19 sts.

Row 9: (For Small) Sc2tog, sc in each st to within 2 sts of marker, sc2tog, sc in center st, sc2tog, sc in each rem st to end of row. Ch 1. Turn. 25 sts.

Row 9: (For Medium) Sc in each st to within 2 sts of marker, sc2tog, sc in center st, sc2tog, sc in each rem st to end of row. Ch 1. Turn. (37) sts.

Row 9: (For Large) Sc in each st across. Ch 1. Turn. 43 sts.

Row 10: (For Small) Sc2tog, sc in each st to within 4 sts of marker, sc2tog 2 times, sc in center st, sc2 tog 2 times, sc in each rem st up to last 2 sts, sc2tog. Fasten off. 19 sts.

Row 10: (For Medium) Sc2tog, sc in each st to within 2 sts of marker, sc2tog, sc in center st, sc2tog, sc in each rem st to end of row. Ch 1. Turn. 33 sts.

Row 10: (For Large) Sc in each st to within 2 sts of marker, sc2tog, sc in center st, sc2tog, sc in each rem st to end of row. Ch 1. Turn. 41 sts.

Row 11: (For Medium and Large) Sc2tog, sc in each st to within 2 sts of marker, sc2tog, sc in center st, sc2tog, sc in each rem st to end of row. Ch 1. Turn. 29 (37) sts.

Row 12: (For Medium) Sc2tog, sc in each st to within 4 sts of marker, sc2tog 2 times, sc in center st, sc2 tog 2 times, sc in each rem st up to last 2 sts, sc2tog. Fasten off. 23 sts.

Row 12: (For Large) Sc2tog, sc in each st to within 2 sts of marker, sc2tog, sc in center st, sc2tog, sc in each rem st to end of row. Ch 1. Turn. 33 sts.

Row 13: (For Large) Sc2tog, sc in each st to within 4 sts of marker, sc2tog 2 times, sc in center st, sc2 tog 2 times, sc in each rem st up to last 2 sts, sc2tog. Fasten off. 27 sts.

Finishing

Weave in all loose ends. Whip stitch center back and foot seam with matching yarn.

Houndtooth Check Boots

Classic style slipper boots you'll love to snuggle in. The slippers in the photo were crocheted using Loops & Threads Charisma bulky weight yarn in Black, White, and Charcoal.

Instructions

Easy / Facile / Fácil

Finished Sizes

Instructions given fit ladies and children's shoe sizes X-small with changes for small, medium, and large in parenthesis. The sizes are color coded for easier reading.

Finished Measurements

Adult - X-Small (3-4) 8 1/2" Small (5-6) 9" Medium (7-8) 9 1/2" Large (9-10) 10"

Children - X-Small (7-8) 6" Small (9-10) 6 1/2" Medium (11-12) 7" Large (1-2) 8"

Materials

Loops & Threads Charisma bulky weight acrylic yarn or any bulky weight yarn. (3.5 oz. / 109 yds / 100g per skein).

Main Color (MC)

Adult - X-Small - 3 oz. / 85g Small - 3.5 oz. / 100g Medium - 3.5 oz. / 100g Large - 5 oz. / 142g

Children - X-Small - 1.5 oz. / 43g Small - 2 oz. / 57g Medium - 2.5 oz. / 71g Large - 3 oz. / 85g

Contrasting Color (CC)

Adult - X-Small - 1.5 oz. / 43g Small - 2 oz. / 57g Medium - 3.0 oz. / 85g Large - 3.0 oz. / 85g

Children - X-Small - 1 oz. / 28g Small - 1 oz. / 28g Medium - 1 oz. / 28g Large - 1.5 oz. / 43g

Notions

Tapestry or yarn needle

Stitch markers

Hook

Size L (8.0 mm) crochet hook or size to obtain gauge.

Gauge

5 sc = 2 inches; 6 sc rows = 2 inches

SPECIAL STITCHES

Single crochet 2 together (sc2tog): Sc2tog means to use single crochet to join two stitches together or decrease by one stitch.

Insert the hook into a stitch and draw up a loop. Insert the hook into the next stitch and draw up a loop. Yarn over, draw through all 3 loops on hook.

PATTERN NOTES

Stitch markers are used to mark the center stitch of the foot rows. To place a marker (PM) first crochet the number of stitches indicated in the pattern, place marker (PM) on the last stitch crocheted, then finish the row as directed. For the following rows move the marker by crocheting up to the stitch just before the marker, remove the marker, crochet the stitch, and then replace the marker.

To change colors in double crochet, yarn over, pull up a loop in the current color you are using, draw through two loops, draw the new color through the last two loops on the hook to complete the double crochet stitch.

In addition to size information being in parenthesis they are color coded to make the patterns easier to read. Numbers and letters in black are for all sizes.

Adult

X-Small   Small   Medium   Large

Children

X-Small   Small   Medium   Large

SLIPPER BOOTS (Make 2)

CUFF (Adult)

Row 1: Ch 23 (25, 27, 29). Sc in 2nd ch from hook, sc in each ch across. Ch 1. Turn. 22 (24, 26, 28) sts.

Rows 2: With MC, sc in 1st st, dc in next st, *sc in next st, dc in next st, rep from * around, ending with a dc. Change to CC in last dc of row. Ch 1. Turn. 22 (24, 26, 28) sts.

Row 3: With CC, sc in 1st st, dc in next st, *sc in next st, dc in next st, rep from * around ending with a dc. Change to MC in last dc of row. Ch 1. Turn. 22 (24, 26, 28) sts.

Rows 4-12: Rep rows 2-3. 22 (24, 27, 29) sts.

CUFF (Children)

Row 1: Ch 19 (19, 21, 23). Sc in 2nd ch from hook, sc in each ch across. Ch 1. Turn. 18 (18, 20, 22) sts.

Rows 2: With MC, sc in 1st st, dc in next st, *sc in next st, dc in next st, rep from * around, ending with a dc. Change to CC in last dc of row. Ch 1. Turn. 18 (18, 20, 22) sts.

Row 3: With CC, sc in 1st st, dc in next st, *sc in next st, dc in next st, rep from * around ending with a dc. Change to MC in last dc of row. Ch 1. Turn 18 (18, 20, 22) sts.

Rows 4-6 (6, 8, 8): Rep rows 2-3. 18 (18, 20, 22) sts.

FOOT (Adult)

Row 1: Sc in first 10 (11, 12, 13) sts, sc2tog, place marker for center st, sc in rem sts. Ch 1. Turn. 21 (23, 25, 27) sts.

Row 2: Sc in each st across. Ch 1. Turn. 21 (23, 25, 27) sts.

Row 3: Sc in each st to within 2 sts of marker, 2 dc in each of the next 2 sts, 5 dc in center st (placing the marker in the 3rd dc), 2 dc in each of next 2 sts, sc in each rem st to end of row. Ch 1. Turn. 29 (31, 33, 35) sts.

Row 4: Sc in each st across. Ch 1. Turn. 29 (31, 33, 35) sts.

Row 5: Rep Row 3. Ch 1. Turn. 37 (39, 41, 43) sts.

Row 6: Sc in each st across. Ch 1. Turn. 37 (39, 41, 43) sts.

Row 7: Rep Row 3. Ch 1. Turn. 45 (47, 49, 51) sts.

Rows 8-8 (9, 10, 11): Rep row 4. Ch 1. Turn. 45 (47, 49, 51) sts.

Rows 9-10 (10-11, 11-12, 12-13): Sc in each st to within 2 sts of marker, sc2tog, sc in center st, sc2tog, sc in each rem st to end of row. Ch 1. Turn. 41 (43, 45, 47) sts.

Row 11 (12, 13, 14): Sc2tog, sc in each st to within 2 sts of marker, sc2tog, sc in center st, sc2 tog, sc in each rem st up to last 2 sts, sc2tog. Ch 1. Turn. 37 (39, 41, 43) sts.

Row 12 (13, 14, 15): Sc2tog, sc in each st to within 4 sts of marker, sc2tog 2 times, sc in center st, sc2 tog 2 times, sc in each rem st up to last 2 sts, sc2tog. Fasten off. 31 (33, 35, 37) sts.

Finishing

Weave in all loose ends. Whip stitch center back and foot seam with matching yarn.

FOOT (Children)

Row 1: Sc in first 8 (8, 9, 10) sts, sc2tog, place marker for center st, sc in rem sts. Ch 1. Turn. 17 (17, 19, 21) sts.

Row 2: Sc in each st across. Ch 1. Turn. 17 (17, 19, 21) sts.

Row 3: 2 sc in first st. Sc in each st to within 1 st of marker, 2 dc in the next st, 5 dc in center st (placing the marker in the 3rd dc), 2 dc in the next st, sc in each rem st to end of row with 2 sc in last st. Ch 1. Turn. 25 (25, 27, 29) sts.

Row 4: Sc in each st across. Ch 1. Turn. 25 (25, 27, 29) sts.

Row 5: (For X-Small and Medium) Sc in each st to within 1 st of marker, 2 dc in the next st, 5 dc in center st (placing the marker in the 3rd dc), 2 dc in the next st, sc in each rem st to end of row. Ch 1. Turn. 31 (33) sts.

Row 5: (For Small and Large) 2 sc in first st. Sc in each st to within 1 st of marker, 2 dc in the next st, 5 dc in center st (placing the marker in the 3rd dc), 2 dc in the next st, sc in each rem st to end of row with 2 sc in last st. Ch 1. Turn. 33 (37) sts.

Row 6: Sc in each st across. Ch 1. Turn. 31 (33, 33, 37) sts.

Row 7: (For X-Small and Small) Sc in each st to within 2 sts of marker, sc2tog, sc in center st, sc2tog, sc in each rem st to end of row. Ch 1. Turn. 29 (31) sts.

Row 7: (For Medium and Large) Sc in each st to within 1 st of marker, 2 dc in the next st, 5 dc in center st (placing the marker in the 3rd dc), 2 dc in the next st, sc in each rem st to end of row. Ch 1. Turn. 39 (43) sts.

Row 8: (For X-Small) Sc2tog, sc in each st to within 2 sts of marker, sc2tog, sc in center st, sc2tog, sc in each rem st to end of row. Ch 1. Turn. 25 sts.

Row 8: (For Small) Sc in each st to within 2 sts of marker, sc2tog, sc in center st, sc2tog, sc in each rem st to end of row. Ch 1. Turn. 29 sts.

Row 8: (For Medium) Sc in each st across. Ch 1. Turn. 39 sts.

Row 8: (For Large) Sc in each st across. Ch 1. Turn. 43 sts.

Row 9: (For X-Small) Sc2tog, sc in each st to within 4 sts of marker, sc2tog 2 times, sc in center st, sc2 tog 2 times, sc in each rem st up to last 2 sts, sc2tog. Fasten off. 19 sts.

Row 9: (For Small) Sc2tog, sc in each st to within 2 sts of marker, sc2tog, sc in center st, sc2tog, sc in each rem st to end of row. Ch 1. Turn. 25 sts.

Row 9: (For Medium) Sc in each st to within 2 sts of marker, sc2tog, sc in center st, sc2tog, sc in each rem st to end of row. Ch 1. Turn. (37) sts.

Row 9: (For Large) Sc in each st across. Ch 1. Turn. 43 sts.

Row 10: (For Small) Sc2tog, sc in each st to within 4 sts of marker, sc2tog 2 times, sc in center st, sc2 tog 2 times, sc in each rem st up to last 2 sts, sc2tog. Fasten off. 19 sts.

Row 10: (For Medium) Sc2tog, sc in each st to within 2 sts of marker, sc2tog, sc in center st, sc2tog, sc in each rem st to end of row. Ch 1. Turn. 33 sts.

Row 10: (For Large) Sc in each st to within 2 sts of marker, sc2tog, sc in center st, sc2tog, sc in each rem st to end of row. Ch 1. Turn. 41 sts.

Row 11: (For Medium and Large) Sc2tog, sc in each st to within 2 sts of marker, sc2tog, sc in center st, sc2tog, sc in each rem st to end of row. Ch 1. Turn. 29 (37) sts.

Row 12: (For Medium) Sc2tog, sc in each st to within 4 sts of marker, sc2tog 2 times, sc in center st, sc2 tog 2 times, sc in each rem st up to last 2 sts, sc2tog. Fasten off. 23 sts.

Row 12: (For Large) Sc2tog, sc in each st to within 2 sts of marker, sc2tog, sc in center st, sc2tog, sc in each rem st to end of row. Ch 1. Turn. 33 sts.

Row 13: (For Large) Sc2tog, sc in each st to within 4 sts of marker, sc2tog 2 times, sc in center st, sc2 tog 2 times, sc in each rem st up to last 2 sts, sc2tog. Fasten off. 27 sts.

Finishing

Weave in all loose ends. Whip stitch center back and foot seam with matching yarn.

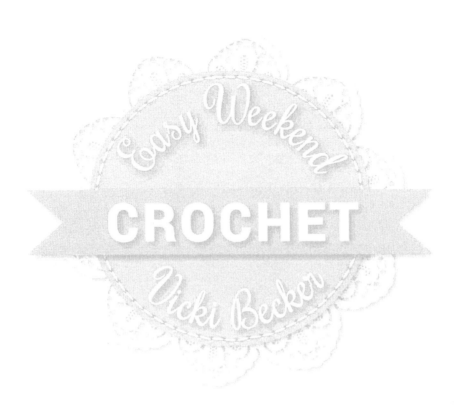

Simply Striped Boots

Simply striped slipper boots can be crocheted using 3 colors or use scrap yarns in as many colors as you like. The slippers in the photo were crocheted using Loops & Threads Charisma bulky weight yarn in Charcoal, White, Think Pink, Espresso, White, and Electric Blue.

Instructions

Easy / Facile / Fácil

Finished Sizes

Instructions given fit ladies and children's shoe sizes X-small with changes for small, medium, and large in parenthesis. The sizes are color coded for easier reading.

Finished Measurements

Adult - X-Small (3-4) 8 1/2" Small (5-6) 9" Medium (7-8) 9 1/2" Large (9-10) 10"

Children - X-Small (7-8) 6" Small (9-10) 6 1/2" Medium (11-12) 7" Large (1-2) 8"

Materials

5 BULKY Loops & Threads Charisma bulky weight acrylic yarn or any bulky weight yarn. (3.5 oz. / 109 yds / 100g per skein).

Main Color (MC)

Adult - X-Small - 3 oz. / 85g Small - 3.5 oz. / 100g Medium - 3.5 oz. / 100g Large - 5 oz. / 142g

Children - X-Small - 1.5 oz. / 43g Small - 2 oz. / 57g Medium - 2.5 oz. / 71g Large - 3 oz. / 85g

Contrasting Colors A and B

Adult - X-Small - 1.5 oz. / 43g Small - 2 oz. / 57g Medium - 3.0 oz. / 85g Large - 3.0 oz. / 85g

Children - X-Small - 1 oz. / 28g Small - 1 oz. / 28g Medium - 1 oz. / 28g Large - 1.5 oz. / 43g

Notions

Tapestry or yarn needle

Stitch markers

Hook

Size L (8.0 mm) crochet hook or size to obtain gauge.

Gauge

5 sc = 2 inches; 6 sc rows = 2 inches

SPECIAL STITCHES

Single crochet 2 together (sc2tog): Sc2tog means to use single crochet to join two stitches together or decrease by one stitch.

Insert the hook into a stitch and draw up a loop. Insert the hook into the next stitch and draw up a loop. Yarn over, draw through all 3 loops on hook.

PATTERN NOTES

Stitch markers are used to mark the center stitch of the foot rows. To place a marker (PM) first crochet the number of stitches indicated in the pattern, place marker (PM) on the last stitch crocheted, then finish the row as directed. For the following rows move the marker by crocheting up to the stitch just before the marker, remove the marker, crochet the stitch, and then replace the marker.

To change colors in double crochet, yarn over, pull up a loop in the current color you are using, draw through two loops, draw the new color through the last two loops on the hook to complete the double crochet stitch.

In addition to size information being in parenthesis they are color coded to make the patterns easier to read. Numbers and letters in black are for all sizes.

Adult

X-Small   Small   Medium   Large

Children

X-Small   Small   Medium   Large

SLIPPER BOOTS (Make 2)

CUFF (Adult)

Row 1: With MC, ch 22 (25, 28, 31). Sc in 2nd ch from hook, sc in each ch across. Change to Color A in last ch of row. Ch 1. Turn. 21 (24, 27, 30) sts.

Rows 2: With Color A, *sc in 1st st, hdc in next st, dc in next st, rep from * around, ending with a dc. Change to Color B in last dc of row. Ch 1. Turn. 21 (24, 27, 30) sts.

Row 3: With Color B, *sc in 1st st, hdc in next st, dc in next st, rep from * around ending with a dc. Change to MC in last dc of row. Ch 1. Turn. 21 (24, 27, 30) sts.

Row 4: With MC, *sc in 1st st, hdc in next st, dc in next st, rep from * around ending with a dc. Change to Color A in last dc of row. Ch 1. Turn. 21 (24, 27, 30) sts.

Rows 5-12: Rep rows 2-4. 21 (24, 27, 30) sts.

CUFF (Children)

Row 1: With MC, ch 19 (19, 22, 22). Sc in 2nd ch from hook, sc in each ch across. Change to Color A in last ch of row. Ch 1. Turn. 18 (18, 21, 21) sts.

Rows 2: With Color A, *sc in 1st st, hdc in next st, dc in next st, rep from * around, ending with a dc. Change to Color B in last dc of row. Ch 1. Turn. 18 (18, 21, 21) sts.

Row 3: With Color B, *sc in 1st st, hdc in next st, dc in next st, rep from * around ending with a dc. Change to MC in last dc of row. Ch 1. Turn. 18 (18, 21, 21) sts.

Row 4: With MC, *sc in 1st st, hdc in next st, dc in next st, rep from * around ending with a dc. Change to Color A in last dc of row. Ch 1. Turn.

Rows 5-6 (6, 8, 8): Rep rows 2-4. 18 (18, 21, 21) sts.

FOOT (Adult)

Row 1: (For X-Small) Sc in first 11 sts, place marker for center st, sc in rem sts. Ch 1. Turn. 21 sts.

Row 1: (For Small) Sc in first 11 sts, sc2tog, place marker for center st, sc in rem sts. Ch 1. Turn. 23 sts.

Row 1: (For Medium) Sc in first 6 sts, sc2 tog, sc in next 6 sts, place marker for center st, sc in next 5 sts, sc2tog, sc in rem sts. Ch 1. Turn. 25 sts.

Row 1: (For Large) Sc in first 7 sts, sc2 tog, sc in next 5 sts, sc2tog, place marker for center st, sc in next 5 sts, sc2tog, sc in rem sts. Ch 1. Turn. 27 sts.

Row 2: Sc in each st across. Ch 1. Turn. 21 (23, 25, 27) sts.

Row 3: Sc in each st to within 2 sts of marker, 2 dc in each of the next 2 sts, 5 dc in center st (placing the marker in the 3rd dc), 2 dc in each of next 2 sts, sc in each rem st to end of row. Ch 1. Turn. 29 (31, 33, 35) sts.

Row 4: Sc in each st across. Ch 1. Turn. 29 (31, 33, 35) sts.

Row 5: Rep Row 3. Ch 1. Turn. 37 (39, 41, 43) sts.

Row 6: Sc in each st across. Ch 1. Turn. 37 (39, 41, 43) sts.

Row 7: Rep Row 3. Ch 1. Turn. 45 (47, 49, 51) sts.

Rows 8-8 (9, 10, 11): Rep row 4. Ch 1. Turn. 45 (47, 49, 51) sts.

Rows 9-10 (10-11, 11-12, 12-13): Sc in each st to within 2 sts of marker, sc2tog, sc in center st, sc2tog, sc in each rem st to end of row. Ch 1. Turn. 41 (43, 45, 47) sts.

Row 11 (12, 13, 14): Sc2tog, sc in each st to within 2 sts of marker, sc2tog, sc in center st, sc2 tog, sc in each rem st up to last 2 sts, sc2tog. Ch 1. Turn. 37 (39, 41, 43) sts.

Row 12 (13, 14, 15): Sc2tog, sc in each st to within 4 sts of marker, sc2tog 2 times, sc in center st, sc2 tog 2 times, sc in each rem st up to last 2 sts, sc2tog. Fasten off. 31 (33, 35, 37) sts.

Finishing

Weave in all loose ends. Whip stitch center back and foot seam with matching yarn.

FOOT (Children)

Row 1: (For X-Small and Small) Sc in first 8 (8) sts, sc2tog, place marker for center st, sc in rem sts. Ch 1. Turn. 17 (17) sts.

Row 1: (For Medium) Sc in first 4 sts, sc2 tog, sc in next 5 sts, place marker for center st, sc in next 4 sts, sc2tog, sc in rem sts. Ch 1. Turn. 19 sts.

Row 1: (For Large) Sc in first 11 sts, place marker for center st, sc in rem sts. Ch 1. Turn. 21 sts.

Row 2: Sc in each st across. Ch 1. Turn. 17 (17, 19, 21) sts.

Row 3: 2 sc in first st. Sc in each st to within 1 st of marker, 2 dc in the next st, 5 dc in center st (placing the marker in the 3rd dc), 2 dc in the next st, sc in each rem st to end of row with 2 sc in last st. Ch 1. Turn. 25 (25, 27, 29) sts.

Row 4: Sc in each st across. Ch 1. Turn. 25 (25, 27, 29) sts.

Row 5: (For X-Small and Medium) Sc in each st to within 1 st of marker, 2 dc in the next st, 5 dc in center st (placing the marker in the 3rd dc), 2 dc in the next st, sc in each rem st to end of row. Ch 1. Turn. 31 (33) sts.

Row 5: (For Small and Large) 2 sc in first st. Sc in each st to within 1 st of marker, 2 dc in the next st, 5 dc in center st (placing the marker in the 3rd dc), 2 dc in the next st, sc in each rem st to end of row with 2 sc in last st. Ch 1. Turn. 33 (37) sts.

Row 6: Sc in each st across. Ch 1. Turn. 31 (33, 33, 37) sts.

Row 7: (For X-Small and Small) Sc in each st to within 2 sts of marker, sc2tog, sc in center st, sc2tog, sc in each rem st to end of row. Ch 1. Turn. 29 (31) sts.

Row 7: (For Medium and Large) Sc in each st to within 1 st of marker, 2 dc in the next st, 5 dc in center st (placing the marker in the 3rd dc), 2 dc in the next st, sc in each rem st to end of row. Ch 1. Turn. 39 (43) sts.

Row 8: (For X-Small) Sc2tog, sc in each st to within 2 sts of marker, sc2tog, sc in center st, sc2tog, sc in each rem st to end of row. Ch 1. Turn. 25 sts.

Row 8: (For Small) Sc in each st to within 2 sts of marker, sc2tog, sc in center st, sc2tog, sc in each rem st to end of row. Ch 1. Turn. 29 sts.

Row 8: (For Medium) Sc in each st across. Ch 1. Turn. 39 sts.

Row 8: (For Large) Sc in each st across. Ch 1. Turn. 43 sts.

Row 9: (For X-Small) Sc2tog, sc in each st to within 4 sts of marker, sc2tog 2 times, sc in center st, sc2 tog 2 times, sc in each rem st up to last 2 sts, sc2tog. Fasten off. 19 sts.

Row 9: (For Small) Sc2tog, sc in each st to within 2 sts of marker, sc2tog, sc in center st, sc2tog, sc in each rem st to end of row. Ch 1. Turn. 25 sts.

Row 9: (For Medium) Sc in each st to within 2 sts of marker, sc2tog, sc in center st, sc2tog, sc in each rem st to end of row. Ch 1. Turn. (37) sts.

Row 9: (For Large) Sc in each st across. Ch 1. Turn. 43 sts.

Row 10: (For Small) Sc2tog, sc in each st to within 4 sts of marker, sc2tog 2 times, sc in center st, sc2 tog 2 times, sc in each rem st up to last 2 sts, sc2tog. Fasten off. 19 sts.

Row 10: (For Medium) Sc2tog, sc in each st to within 2 sts of marker, sc2tog, sc in center st, sc2tog, sc in each rem st to end of row. Ch 1. Turn. 33 sts.

Row 10: (For Large) Sc in each st to within 2 sts of marker, sc2tog, sc in center st, sc2tog, sc in each rem st to end of row. Ch 1. Turn. 41 sts.

Row 11: (For Medium and Large) Sc2tog, sc in each st to within 2 sts of marker, sc2tog, sc in center st, sc2tog, sc in each rem st to end of row. Ch 1. Turn. 29 (37) sts.

Row 12: (For Medium) Sc2tog, sc in each st to within 4 sts of marker, sc2tog 2 times, sc in center st, sc2 tog 2 times, sc in each rem st up to last 2 sts, sc2tog. Fasten off. 23 sts.

Row 12: (For Large) Sc2tog, sc in each st to within 2 sts of marker, sc2tog, sc in center st, sc2tog, sc in each rem st to end of row. Ch 1. Turn. 33 sts.

Row 13: (For Large) Sc2tog, sc in each st to within 4 sts of marker, sc2tog 2 times, sc in center st, sc2 tog 2 times, sc in each rem st up to last 2 sts, sc2tog. Fasten off. 27 sts.

Finishing

Weave in all loose ends. Whip stitch center back and foot seam with matching yarn.

More Needlework Books by Vicki Becker

Available exclusively at Amazon.com for kindle and in paperback.
http://www.amazon.com/-/e/B009ZWK7Q6

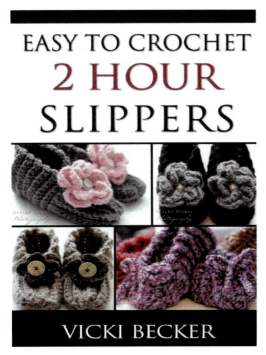

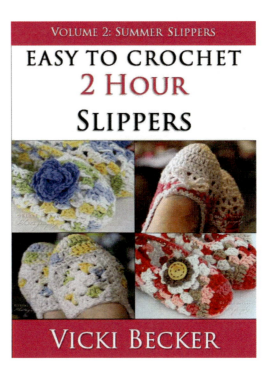

Easy To Crochet 2 Hour Slippers

http://www.amazon.com/gp/product/B00AXQO840

These cute slippers are very easy and quick to make. You can crochet these slippers in about 2 hours depending on how fast you crochet using bulky yarn and a J, K, or L hook.

Easy To Crochet 2 Hour Slippers Volume 2

http://www.amazon.com/gp/product/B00D5FH1QI

These cute slippers are very quick and easy to make. The designs use cotton yarns for cool comfortable slippers. The pattern instructions are for 4 different styles of ladies slippers in three sizes.

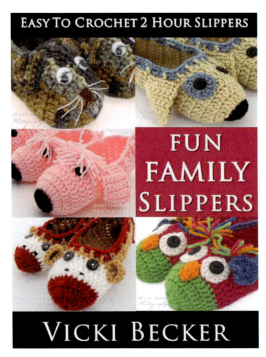 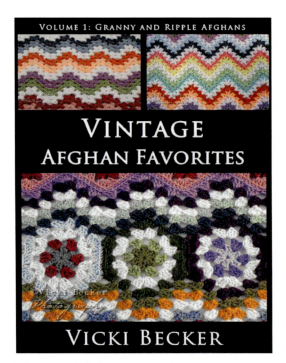

Easy To Crochet 2 Hour Slippers Volume 2

http://www.amazon.com/gp/product/B00E8OW3BS

These cute slippers are very quick and easy to make. The designs use #4 medium weight yarns. The cute puppies, colorful owls, pink poodles, calico cats, and mischievous sock monkeys are all great for gift giving.

Vintage Afghan Favorites

http://www.amazon.com/gp/product/B00FI6K1ZU

When you think about vintage afghans the granny probably is the first afghan that comes to mind and then the classic ripple. In this book I have put a new twist on these two vintage afghan styles. The four afghans in this book are my interpretation of these classic designs.

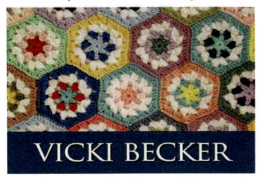
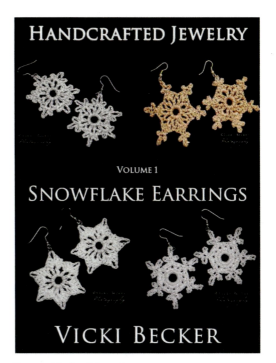

Easy To Crochet Vintage Scrap Afghans

http://www.amazon.com/gp/product/B009P7Q2KG

Get out your odds and ends of yarn! All these afghans can be made with scrap yarn! Not only are they vintage beauties they are economical too.

Snowflake Earrings

http://www.amazon.com/gp/product/B00HM9BY2A

These delicate snowflake earrings make up fast. The patterns use a size 10 metallic crochet thread

And size 5 (1.9mm) steel crochet hook. There are 4 designs for snowflake earrings.

Easy To Crochet 2 Hour Slippers Volume 2

http://www.amazon.com/gp/product/B00N4FQ1C4

Vintage lace earrings are so quick and easy you can crochet a pair in two hours or less! The patterns, however, are for more experienced crocheters as the earrings are made with crochet thread and small hooks.

Easy To Crochet Sweeper & Duster Covers

http://www.amazon.com/gp/product/B00BXTYBH0

You can crochet your own reusable Eco friendly sweeper and duster covers. Why pay for expensive disposable refills when you can make these great covers for a fraction of the cost? They are quick to make and easy care. Simply toss them in the washer and dryer!

Christmas Crochet Coffee Cup Cozies

http://www.amazon.com/gp/product/B00H7JPESU

Crochet these quick and easy Christmas coffee cup cozies for yourself or to give as a gift. The coffee cozies can be made up in less than an hour and make great last minute gifts. Cheerful and bright in colorful Christmas colors or make them in any color you wish.

Christmas Crochet Snowflakes

http://www.amazon.com/gp/product/B00HFH961U

Quick and easy thread ornaments for your Christmas tree or to use as package toppers. The patterns use a size 5 crochet thread and D crochet hook so you can make them in a hurry! There are 8 designs for snowflakes.

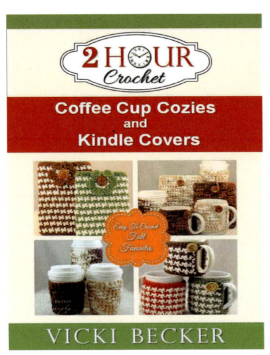

2 Hour Crochet: Easy To Crochet Coffee Cup Cozies and Kindle Covers

http://www.amazon.com/gp/product/B00OBQSTGQ

Coffee cozies and kindle covers are so quick and easy you can crochet one in two hours or less! The patterns are easy, however, you should know how to crochet in the round and be able to front and back post crochet before attempting these patterns.

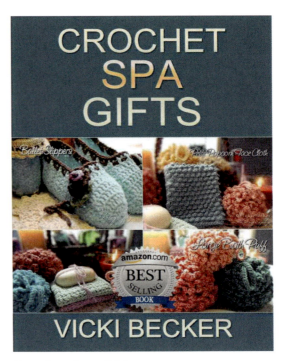

Crochet Spa Gifts

http://www.amazon.com/gp/product/B00A11DBTA

You can create your own crocheted spa gift sets for Christmas gifts, birthdays, or any special occasion!

Instructions are for a small and large bath puff made from Caron's Spa yarn.

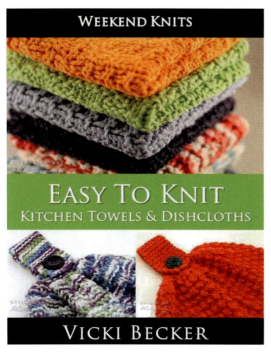 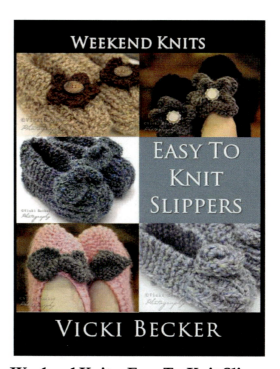

Weekend Knits: Easy To Knit Kitchen Towels & Dishcloths

http://www.amazon.com/gp/product/B00M5PZVB6

These hanging kitchen towels and dishcloths are quick and easy to make. You can knit a set in just a weekend using cotton yarns and number 9 knitting needles.

Weekend Knits: Easy To Knit Slippers

http://www.amazon.com/gp/product/B00GWTYPOA

These warm and cuddly slippers are very quick and easy to make. You can knit these slippers in just a weekend using #5 and #6 bulky yarns. The pattern instructions are for 3 different style slippers in three sizes. Two of the pattern instructions are written for different types of yarn so there are actually 5 slipper patterns in all.

Quick and Easy Crochet: Plant Hangers

http://www.amazon.com/gp/product/B0128LZRYW

Crochet plant hangers make beautiful and unique gifts or a wonderful addition to your own home decor. These wonderful plant hangers are easy to crochet and quick to make! They're great for indoor or outdoor use as the nylon is very durable and does not fade or rot.

Coloring Book Crafts: Vintage Flowers Rag Quilt & Pillow

http://www.amazon.com/gp/product/B018DE8J5C

Vintage Flowers Rag Quilt and Pillow is a book that combines coloring with quilting and embroidery. Coloring allows you to explore your creativity and is very relaxing, but you can do so much more than just color on paper! The Coloring Book Craft series will take your love of coloring to a whole new level!

http://www.amazon.com/gp/product/B01BHBHF0U

Slipper Boots is the first book in the Easy Weekend Crochet series. These crocheted slippers are quick and easy projects that you can complete in a weekend or less. Slipper boots keep your feet warm and toasty and are perfect for lounging and snuggling. Crochet these comfy cozy boots for yourself or as a gift for someone special.

Conclusion

I hope you enjoyed the patterns. Please consider leaving me a review. I value your opinion and would love to hear from you.

You can also visit my face book fan page to leave a message or comment.

http://www.facebook.com/VickiBeckerAuthor

Visit my author page at Amazon for a list of my other needlework titles!

http://www.amazon.com/-/e/B009ZWK7Q6

Visit my web site for more needlework tips and patterns!

http://easyweekendcrochet.com

You can email me

vicki@easyweekendcrochet.com

Made in the USA
Columbia, SC
02 November 2020